6-12-16

Dear Hans, Laurie & Family.
I hope this devotional would be part of Daily Lives

40 Days in the Word:

A Daily Devotional

Love
Beatriz

Monica Johnson

Copyright © 2012 by Monica Johnson

Printed in the United States of America

mmjohnso@pacbell.net

All Rights Reserved Worldwide. No portion of this book may be reproduced, stored in a retrieval system or transmitted in any form or by any means – electronic, photocopy, recording, scanning or other – except for brief quotations in critical reviews, articles or books, without prior written permission of the author or publisher.

ISBN-13: 978-0615688527
ISBN-10: 0615688527

ISBN information is registered with BooksInPrint.com[A®]

Scripture Quotations
Any bold highlighting or italics of Scriptures are emphasis added by the author of this book.

All scripture quotations, unless otherwise indicated, are taken from the Holy Bible, New International Version®, NIV®. Copyright ©1973, 1978, 1984, 2011 by Biblica, Inc.™ Used by permission of Zondervan. All rights reserved worldwide.
www.zondervan.com

The "NIV" and "New International Version" are trademarks registered in the United States Patent and Trademark Office by Biblica, Inc.™

Book cover and layout by Brad and Monica Johnson
Cover photo by Brad Johnson

Table of Contents

Acknowledgements…..………………i

Introduction…………………………ii

Day 1…………………………….…...1

Day 2……………………………..…..2

Day 3…..………………………….….3

Day 4…..…………………………..…4

Day 5……………………………..…..5

Day 6…..……………………….…….6

Day 7…..………………………….….7

Day 8…..………………………….….9

Day 9…..………………………..…..11

Day 10…..………………………..….12

Day 11……………………...………..15

Day 12…..……………………………17

Day 13…....…………………………..18

Day 14…..……………………………19

Day 15…..……………………………21

Day 16…..……………………………22

Day 17…..……………………………23

Day 18…..……………………………25

Day 19…..……………………………27

Day 20…...……………………………29

Day 21………………………………...31
Day 22…… …………………………33
Day 23…..………………………….35
Day 24…..………………………….37
Day 25…..………………………….39
Day 26…..………………………….41
Day 27……...……………………….43
Day 28…..………………………….45
Day 29…..………………………….47
Day 30…..………………………….49
Day 31…...………………………….51
Day 32…..………………………….53
Day 3…..………………………….55
Day 34…..………………………….57
Day 35…..………………………….59
Day 36…...………………………….61
Day 37…..………………………….63
Day 38…..………………………….65
Day 39…..………………………….67
Day 40…..………………………….69
Closing Thoughts…………………..71
Additional Reading…………....……74

Acknowledgments

First, I am so thankful to my Savior, Jesus Christ. Because of Him, I am a new creation. Jesus said in the Gospel of John, *"No one can come to me unless the Father who sent me draws them, and I will raise them up at the last day. It is written in the Prophets: 'They will all be taught by God. Everyone who has heard the Father and learned from him comes to me (John 6:44-45)."* I am so thankful for my mother who gave me my faith in God and it was through this foundation that I ultimately came into the saving knowledge of Jesus. I'm truly blessed that the Lord made her my mother – she has modeled great faith and has always supported and encouraged me.

I also want to thank my amazing husband, Brad, who is so supportive of all that I do. It is such a blessing to share our love of the Lord and to see together how God has orchestrated events in our lives that have brought great blessings. When we've trusted in Him, even when there was no earthly evidence to, He has always exceeded our expectations. I'm thankful to have the privilege of having such a wonderful man of God as my husband! I'm thankful too for his mom (my second mom) and her faith that she has shared with us over the years.

I'm thankful for my amazing church family and for my pastor, Dwight Bailey, Jr. It is within this community that I have seen the love of the Father manifested and my relationship with Him has been strengthened by this fellowship. (*In the same way, let your light shine before others, that they may see your good deeds and glorify your Father in heaven (Matthew 5:16).* I apologize ahead of time that space does not permit me to thank so many people personally who have been such blessings to my family and me.

I am also thankful for my dear friend and spiritual mentor, Sandy Petersen, who has walked with me through some difficult times and always held me up with her friendship and spiritual encouragement. She is a great blessing to me.

I'm thankful too for Ginny Kisling's support and help with getting this book to print. Her help has been invaluable to this process.

I also want to thank my son for the incredible young man he is and for his big faith. It's amazing how he has encouraged me even from an early age.

Every good and perfect gift is from above, coming down from the Father of the heavenly lights, who does not change like shifting shadows. – James 1:17

Thank you, Lord, for all of your wonderful gifts to me!

Introduction

When I was in my early teens, my friend and I used to go to the park and swing on the swings. I used to love to swing since it was there I felt a reprieve from some of the difficult circumstances I encountered growing up. I remember swinging and telling my friend that one day I would write a book. I felt that I had already experienced so many things that seemed so different than many people I knew (challenges that sometimes felt overwhelming) that perhaps I would have a story to tell – a story that might help someone else some day.

As the years went on, I continued to have this stirring that I was supposed to write a book, but I never knew when that would be.

I was raised going to church every week. As I struggled through those difficult years of growing up (my father left when I was 8, my brother struggled with many problems that affected the family, financial problems, depression, etc.), it was my mom's faith in God and my own faith that got me through. I remember even from an early age that I felt a strong sense of the presence of God, even though I would go onto some difficult times and choices that didn't allow for me to experience the peace and freedom of walking closely with Him. However, He was always there. He was just waiting for me to come to Him and bring everything to Him – even the things I thought I could manage better than He could – so He could give me that peace I so desperately needed.

At a very difficult time in my early adulthood I remember looking up at the ceiling and saying, "Okay, God, I give up. You take my life and do with it what you want. I haven't been able to do it my way – I've made a mess – so I surrender to you." I'll never forget the peace I had that night. It truly was a beginning of my way up and out of the pit.

There would still be more years before I would actually come into the relationship that I now share with my Savior. However, as I look back, I see all the ways He drew me to Him and never gave up on me. In His mercy and grace, He would reveal more and more to me about who is He – as much as I wanted to know – and what He wanted me to know about myself. Of course, this is a process that continues and will not be complete this side of Heaven. I have come to treasure above all else my relationship with Him, and it's my desire that everyone I know could experience the gift that only He can give.

Last year, I ended up writing some devotionals for my church during the Lenten season. I felt the Lord had put this on my heart and when I wrote, strangely, it didn't feel like work at all, which is unusual for me. When I was finished, I had 40 days of devotions and realized that I had a book! Isn't it interesting how God works?

I pray this book will encourage you and will allow you to see how much God loves you and to what great lengths He went to in order to give you life – abundant life – both now and forever.

Day 1

Jesus answered, "It is written: 'Man shall not live on bread alone, but on every word that comes from the mouth of God.' - Matthew 4:4.

Just like we need food to nourish our bodies and to fortify us, we need our Lord Jesus (the Word) to nourish, sustain and fortify our souls. It is imperative, as Christians, that we learn God's Word and that we feed on it daily. It is our sustenance, our protection, our life.

Prayer: Father, we thank you for your Son, we thank you for your Word. Helps us to grow deeper in our relationship with you by feeding more and more on your Holy Word and walking ever closer with you. In Jesus' name we pray, Amen.

Day 2

For he will command his angels concerning you to guard you in all your ways; they will lift you up in their hands, so that you will not strike your foot against a stone. - Psalm 91: 11-12. Do not put the LORD your God to the test as you did at Massah - Deuteronomy 6:16

Just as Jesus totally trusted His Father, we are to do the same. Our God instructs us not to test Him, and we don't need to. In His sovereignty and goodness, He alone knows what we need, and He is able to accomplish it. When we are fully surrendered to Him and His will, He is able to do exceedingly more than all we could hope or ask for.

Prayer: Father, we thank you for who you are. We thank you that you can be trusted at all times and in all circumstances. We ask that we are ever mindful of your goodness and trustworthiness. In Jesus' name we pray, Amen.

Day 3

Fear the LORD your God, serve him only… - Deuteronomy 6:13.

This may seem simple enough, but there are many things that can become idols for us. We are to serve Him only. Just as our Lord said, "No one can serve two masters. Either he will hate the one and love the other, or he will be devoted to the one and despise the other (Matthew 6:24.)."

Prayer: Lord, we thank you that no temptation has overtaken us that is not common to man, and that you are faithful, and you will not let us be tempted beyond our ability, but with the temptation, you will also provide the way of escape, that we may be able to endure it. Help us, Lord, to flee from idolatry and to only serve you - our King of Kings and Lord of Lords! In Jesus' name we pray, Amen.

Day 4

For God so loved the world that he gave his one and only Son, that whoever believes in him shall not perish but have eternal life - John 3:16. For Christ also suffered once for sins, the righteous for the unrighteous, to bring you to God - 1 Peter 3:18.

What an amazing thing! God loves us so much that He gave us His one and only Son, and all He asks is that we believe in Him! Our perfect Lord, righteous and completely holy, suffered for our sins so that we could be brought to God. What other story in all of humanity compares to this? What other religion offers this?

Prayer: Wonderful, amazing, God! How blessed are we that our Creator is so loving and merciful! We fall on our knees in awe and praise of you! Thank you for the greatest gift to mankind - your precious Son! We thank you that through Him we will have eternal life. In Jesus' most holy name we pray, Amen.

Day 5

The fear of the LORD is pure, enduring forever. The decrees of the LORD are firm, and all of them are righteous. They are more precious than gold, than much pure gold; they are sweeter than honey, than honey from the honeycomb. By them your servant is warned; in keeping them there is great reward - Psalm 19: 9-11.

For the unbeliever, the fear of the Lord is the fear of the judgment of God and eternal death - separation from God. For the believer, the fear of God is something different. Believers are not to be afraid of God. We have His promise that nothing can separate us from His love (Romans 8:38-39), and we have His promise that He will never leave us or forsake us (Hebrews 13:5). However, we are to be in awe of Him and have reverence for Him. Fearing God is respecting Him, obeying Him, submitting to His correction, and worshiping Him in awe.

Prayer: Lord, we stand in awe of you! We thank you that you are mighty and holy and that your ways are righteous. We ask that you continue to plant your Word in us so that we will know how to live a life that is pleasing to you. We ask this in Jesus' name, Amen.

Day 6

Then the King will say to those on his right, 'Come, you who are blessed by my Father; take your inheritance, the kingdom prepared for you since the creation of the world. For I was hungry and you gave me something to eat, I was thirsty and you gave me something to drink, I was a stranger and you invited me in, I needed clothes and you clothed me, I was sick and you looked after me, I was in prison and you came to visit me.' - Matthew 25:34-36.

Our Lord is a God of compassion and mercy. He told us that the two most important commandments are to love the Lord with your whole heart, with your whole soul and with all your mind and to love your neighbor as yourself. Our Christian walk is not to be one that only concerns our needs. We are to show the love of our Lord and Savior by doing acts of service, love and mercy toward others.

Prayer: Lord, we thank you that you are a merciful and loving God. We ask that you keep our hearts and our eyes open as we go about our day so that we may be available to the needs of this hurting world. We ask for divine appointments so that we may show your love to others. We ask this in Jesus' precious name, Amen.

Day 7

For this reason, ever since I heard about your faith in the Lord Jesus and your love for all God's people, I have not stopped giving thanks for you, remembering you in my prayers. I keep asking that the God of our Lord Jesus Christ, the glorious Father, may give you the Spirit] of wisdom and revelation, so that you may know him better. I pray that the eyes of your heart may be enlightened in order that you may know the hope to which he has called you, the riches of his glorious inheritance in his holy people, and his incomparably great power for us who believe. – Ephesians 1 15-19.

What an amazing prayer that Paul is praying on behalf of his friends. First, he prays that they be given the Spirit of wisdom and revelation that they may know Him better. We too need this prayer. Second, he prays that the eyes of their hearts may be enlightened so they would know the hope in which He called them, the riches of His inheritance for His people (us who believe) and the power for all who believe. We have so much as Christians – those who call Jesus

Christ their Lord and Savior – and yet we often are blinded to these blessings and riches. We too need to pray for others, and ourselves, these things that Paul prays so that we will be able to live the victorious life our Savior would have us live.

Prayer: Lord, we thank you for your Word and for this prayer of Paul's that is a powerful prayer for all of us in any age. We too want to know you better and want the eyes of our heart to be open and in tune with all that you've done for us, prepared for us, and the power that you extend to us as your followers. We pray for more and more understanding and knowledge of you – our greatest treasure, our King of kings and Lord of Lords! We ask this in the mighty name of Jesus, Amen.

Day 8

All this is from God, who reconciled us to himself through Christ and gave us the ministry of reconciliation: that God was reconciling the world to himself in Christ, not counting people's sins against them. And he has committed to us the message of reconciliation. We are therefore Christ's ambassadors, as though God were making his appeal through us. We implore you on Christ's behalf: Be reconciled to God. God made him who had no sin to be sin for us, so that in him we might become the righteousness of God. – 2 Corinthians 5:18-21

Merriam-Webster dictionary defines reconcile as "to restore to friendship or harmony." In the above passage, Paul tells us how God was reconciling the world to Himself in Christ, not counting people's sins against them. We have all sinned and fallen short of God's glory, yet He reaches out to us, offers us reconciliation and doesn't count these sins against us. However, the only way to receive this reconciliation is by believing and receiving Jesus Christ as our Savior. God is holy, sovereign, omnipotent, omniscient, and omnipresent. It is His prerogative to do as He pleases and that could include offering the punishment that we all deserve; however, in His grace and mercy, He offers us reconciliation through the gift of His Son, Jesus. How is it that anyone could refuse this gift?

Prayer: We thank you, Lord, for your love for us and your desire to be reconciled with us - your creation who has stumbled and sinned before you. We thank you that you understand our condition and have offered us a way out. We ask that you would help us to be the ambassadors of goodwill that you want us to be for your Kingdom – offering the Good News of Jesus Christ to all we can so that they too will know of your love and mercy towards them. We ask this in Jesus' name, Amen.

Day 9

Whoever believes in the Son of God accepts this testimony. Whoever does not believe God has made him out to be a liar, because they have not believed the testimony God has given about his Son. And this is the testimony: God has given us eternal life, and this life is in his Son. Whoever has the Son has life; whoever does not have the Son of God does not have life. – I John 5:11-12

The above passage makes it pretty clear that if a person does not have Jesus Christ, they won't have eternal life with God. There is no human being who has ever lived, other than Jesus Christ, who died and then three days later came back to life and was seen by hundreds. Some of these people who were eyewitnesses to His death and resurrection went on to record these facts for the generations to come and were even willing to die for what they knew to be true. Jesus Himself said regarding God, "I and the Father are one (John 10:30)." There are a lot of religions in the world, but there is only one that is true. Jesus Himself tells us through His Word, "I am the way and the truth and the life. No one comes to the

Father except through me (John 14:6)." If we don't believe Him, we don't believe God, which pretty much says we think God is a liar. The truth is God has spoken, Jesus Christ is our Savior, and if we don't accept this, we won't have eternal life with Him. God Himself became a man and took the sins of the world on Him. It's our choice to accept this.

Prayer: Thank you Lord, for the gift of your Son, Jesus. We accept the truth of who He is, and We ask Him to be the Lord and Savior of our lives. Thank you for all that you've done for us and the great lengths you went to in saving your lost world. We believe your Words, and we thank you that when we believe in our hearts and confess with our mouths that Jesus Christ is Lord, we are saved. We pray that you would remove the scales from the eyes of those who do not believe this Truth and we ask that you would help us in leading others to your Truth. In Jesus' name we pray, Amen.

Day 10

But who can discern their own errors? Forgive my hidden faults. Keep your servant also from willful sins; may they not rule over me. Then I will be blameless, innocent of great transgression. May these words of my mouth and this meditation of my heart be pleasing in your sight, LORD, my Rock and my Redeemer. – Psalm 19: 12-14

Isn't it amazing that we can think we see so clearly other people's faults but often are blind to our own? Jesus told us, "How can you say to your brother, 'Let me take the speck out of your eye,' when all the time there is a plank in your own eye? You hypocrite, first take the plank out of your own eye, and then you will see clearly to remove the speck from your brother's eye (Matthew 7:4-5)." How do we actually take that plank out? We take it out by going to our Lord. He is the One that can help us see what we can't. He is the One who can forgive our hidden faults. He also, if we ask, can keep us from those willful sins that are so hard to break so that they don't have to rule over us. How much better would things be if we started each day by asking the Lord to make the words of our mouths and the meditations of our hearts be pleasing to Him? How about if we asked every hour?

Prayer: Lord, we thank you for your mercy. We thank you that you are here to offer us help in this sinful, broken world. We all have faults that are both known and even unknown to us, and we ask that you lovingly show us these things and help us to overcome them. We reach out to you and ask that you would help us with those willful sins that are often so hard to break. However, we know we can have victory through you, Lord! May the words of our mouths and the meditations of our hearts truly be pleasing to you! We ask this in the precious, mighty name of our Lord and Savior, Jesus Christ, Amen.

Day 11

Be merciful, just as your Father is merciful. "Do not judge, and you will not be judged. Do not condemn, and you will not be condemned. Forgive, and you will be forgiven. Give, and it will be given to you. A good measure, pressed down, shaken together and running over, will be poured into your lap. For with the measure you use, it will be measured to you." - Luke 6:36-38

Like many of Jesus' commands, this one requires that we stay close to Him, the Vine, in order for us to carry this out. We judge and condemn for so many reasons. Often our judgments come out of our own hurts and insecurities. We fail to forgive because we feel so slighted. However, we need to remember our Savior, who was completely humble and not prideful in any way, as we seek to overlook offenses, not judge another person's heart or motivations, etc. Only our God can know the motivations and heart of another. When we think we know this, we are stepping into territory that does not, and never has, belonged to us.

Prayer: Father, we repent before you that we have often judged and condemned others. We ask that you forgive us and that your Holy Spirit will continue to work in us to help us as we live a life of daily surrender and dependence on you. We ask that you would help us take every thought captive to the obedience of Christ and that we would release to you whatever relationships or circumstances are causing us to act or think in a way that is contrary to you. In Jesus' name we pray, Amen.

Day 12

The greatest among you will be your servant. For those who exalt themselves will be humbled, and those who humble themselves will be exalted - Matthew 23:11-12

In the 23 chapter of Matthew's Gospel, Jesus warns of hypocrisy. As we read this passage, we may be thinking what hypocrites the Pharisees were and, perhaps, are appalled at their behavior - thinking we would never do what they did. However, there are times in our lives when we too are hypocrites. Let us be mindful of the possibility of hypocrisy in our lives and ask our Lord to reveal to us areas where we may be hypocritical.

Prayer: Father, we ask that you search our hearts and reveal to us any hidden sin that we need to examine. We ask that in your grace, you would lovingly show us areas where we too have been hypocritical. We ask that you forgive us and lead us anew in a path that recognizes this tendency and seeks to choose instead to see that we are all broken and in need of a savior. In Jesus' name we pray, Amen.

Day 13

Then *a cloud appeared and covered them, and a voice came from the cloud: "This is my Son, whom I love. Listen to him! - Mark 9:7*

Jesus was transfigured on a high mountain top before Peter, James and John. The words that they heard from our glorious Father in heaven are words that we are to still follow today - "Listen to Him!" Whether it is from reading His word or through listening to His whispers in our hearts, we are to listen and obey our Lord and Master, Jesus Christ.

Prayer: Lord, we are so thankful for you. We praise you that you have given us eternal life through your Son and that you have also given us a road map for our lives through your Word. We ask that you quicken our hearts and minds so that we would listen to you and be doers of your Word - not just hearers. In Jesus' name we pray, Amen.

Day 14

What, then, shall we say in response to these things? If God is for us, who can be against us? He who did not spare his own Son, but gave him up for us all—how will he not also, along with him, graciously give us all things? Who will bring any charge against those whom God has chosen? It is God who justifies. Who then is the one who condemns? No one. Christ Jesus who died—more than that, who was raised to life—is at the right hand of God and is also interceding for us. - Romans 8:31-34

Wow, if God is for us, who can be against us? That is powerful! How amazing also that our Lord and Savior, Jesus Christ, is at the right hand of God interceding for us! We have one intercessor between God and man and that is Jesus himself. Because of His work on the cross, we can come before the throne of God and lay our burdens down before Him.

Prayer: We thank you and praise you our Holy Triune God! We thank you Father for giving us your son. We thank you Jesus that you love us so much that you laid down your life for us. We thank you Holy Spirit that you are working in us to will and to act in order to fulfill God's good purpose. We pray, Lord, that you will continue to work in us in such a way that we will fully embrace what the gift of you in our lives' means and we will lay everything before you, being fully transparent in all ways, so that we can receive the blessings you intend for us and you would be glorified. In Jesus' most holy name we pray, Amen.

Day 15

No longer will they teach their neighbor, or say to one another, 'Know the LORD,' because they will all know me, from the least of them to the greatest," declares the LORD. "For I will forgive their wickedness and will remember their sins no more. – Jeremiah 31:34

There will come a time when every knee will bow before Jesus and every tongue shall confess to God that Jesus Christ is Lord. How wonderful that Jesus Christ already gained victory for us over death and this world and because of this, our sins will not be remembered by Him. As we look towards the coming of our Savior, it is crucially important that we give everyone the chance to know about God's redemption through His Son. Jesus said that we are to love the Lord our God with all are our heart, with all our mind and will all our soul and to love our neighbor as ourselves. What better way to love others than to point them to the One who is love?

Prayer: Father, we look forward to that day when every knee will bow before you and give Jesus, our King, the honor that He deserves. We ask that you would give us a boldness to preach your gospel to this hurting world. We know that it's not your will that any should perish but that all should come to repentance. Thank you for the honor of being part of your Kingdom work. We ask this in Jesus' name, Amen.

Day 16

Because I have sinned against him, I will bear the LORD's wrath, until he pleads my case and upholds my cause. He will bring me out into the light; I will see his righteousness. – Micah 7:19

The truth is that we all have sinned and fallen short of the glory of God. We all are deserving of God's wrath. However, in His kindness and mercy He made a way of escape for us – the way of His beloved Son and His shed blood for us. Jesus is the true Light of the world and it is because of Him that we are righteous. Jesus Christ is our righteousness.

Prayer: Thank you, Lord, for your kindness and your mercy. We thank you that when we put our hope and trust in you as our Savior, our sins our forgiven. We thank you that you do not treat us as our sins deserve - as far as the east is from the west so far have you removed our transgressions from us. We ask that you would keep this truth ever before us so that we can truly appreciate the gift that we have in you. We ask this in Jesus' precious name, Amen.

Day 17

Now faith is confidence in what we hope for and assurance about what we do not see. This is what the ancients were commended for. – Hebrews 11: 1-2; And without faith it is impossible to please God, because anyone who comes to him must believe that he exists and that he rewards those who earnestly seek him. – Hebrews 11:6

God's Word tell us that it is by grace we have been saved – through faith, which is a gift from God. We have to exercise this faith, though. As the scriptures above mention, the ancients were commended for their faith and without faith it is impossible to please God. Jesus talks about the importance of faith, and that when we have real faith, mountains can be moved. We often encounter mountains in our lives or things that seem impossible. However, our God is the God of the impossible. Let us stand firm in our faith. Our Lord and Savior tells us, "Everything is possible for one who believes." (Mark 9:23)

Prayer: Father, we thank you for your gift of faith. We ask that you would strengthen our faith in you. Just as the man who brought his son to be healed by you, Lord, said that he believed but asked that you would help him overcome his unbelief, we too ask that you would help us to overcome our unbelief wherever it exists. In Jesus' name we pray, Amen.

Day 18

Now when Jesus saw the crowds, he went up on a mountainside and sat down. His disciples came to him, and he began to teach them. He said: "Blessed are the poor in spirit, for theirs is the kingdom of heaven. Blessed are those who mourn, for they will be comforted. Blessed are the meek, for they will inherit the earth. Blessed are those who hunger and thirst for righteousness, for they will be filled. Blessed are the merciful, for they will be shown mercy. Blessed are the pure in heart, for they will see God. Blessed are the peacemakers, for they will be called children of God. Blessed are those who are persecuted because of righteousness, for theirs is the kingdom of heaven. – Matthew 5:1-10

Jesus' words in His Sermon on the Mount to His disciples are words for us today as well. In each of our Lord's statements, he begins with the word "Blessed". When we walk in God's will there are many blessings to be had. The economy of God's kingdom is different than the economy of this world. To be poor in spirit is to recognize your great spiritual need and to depend on God to meet that need. When we mourn our sinfulness and brokenness, our merciful Savior comforts us. When we are meek and humble before Him, He rewards us with the inheritance he promised Abraham. Basically, in all of these "Blessed" statements, we are given instructions on how we can be blessed and receive what the Lord has prepared for us - His children - who follow after Him, worship Him and obey Him.

Prayer: Father, thank you for the many blessings you have for us. Thank you for the way you lead us and guide us. Your Word tells us that our citizenship is in heaven. We are eagerly awaiting the return of our King – Jesus Christ - from there who will transform us. Father, help us to be in the world but not of the world. Keep our eyes ever focused on you and your heavenly kingdom. In Jesus' name we pray, Amen.

Day 19

He was delivered over to death for our sins and was raised to life for our justification – Romans 4:25; "Therefore, since we have been justified through faith, we have peace with God through our Lord Jesus Christ" – Romans 5:1

Wow, we have been justified before the God of the universe because we believe in His Son, Jesus Christ, and accept his sacrifice for the payment of our sins! Really, that's all it takes to be justified before God? The answer is an astounding, "Yes!" His Word tells us that righteousness from God comes through faith in Jesus Christ to all who believe (Romans 3:22). Our God is a just God, and sins that are committed cannot be unpunished. However, because of His mercy and love, our Savior paid the price for our sins and allows us to be seen by God as righteous because He sees His righteous Son when he looks at us who believe in His Son. Because of this justification, we can have assurance of our salvation. Once we accept His free gift of justification and salvation, He can start to do the work in us that makes us become more like His son in our words, thoughts and deeds – the process of sanctification.

Prayer: Lord, we thank you that because of your Son and our belief in Him, we are justified before you. We ask that you help us to never minimize the importance of this amazing gift. We ask that, through your Holy Spirit, we will be able to see our lives the way you see them and that we will accept the guidance you give us in order to make us into the people you would have us become. In Jesus' name we pray, Amen.

Day 20

Praise be to the God and Father of our Lord Jesus Christ! In his great mercy he has given us new birth into a living hope through the resurrection of Jesus Christ from the dead, and into an inheritance that can never perish, spoil or fade. This inheritance is kept in heaven for you, who through faith are shielded by God's power until the coming of the salvation that is ready to be revealed in the last time. In all this you greatly rejoice, though now for a little while you may have had to suffer grief in all kinds of trials. – 1 Peter 1:3-6

On planet Earth we have all kinds of trials and troubles. In fact, our Lord told us that in the world we would have trouble, but to take heart because He has overcome the world. How amazing that God's power is shielding us and keeping us until that great day when we are with Him! Life is a gift from our Creator and while there are hardships and troubles, there are blessings and beauty as well. And, when we are finished with this life, we have the gift of everlasting life with Him where there will be no more trials or tears.

Prayer: Father, thank you for all the ways you shield us and keep us. Thank you, Lord, for the gift of eternal life with you through our Savior, Jesus. We ask that you help us keep the perspective we need in battling life's trials, knowing that you are with us and that we need to enjoy every moment since life does, indeed, go by so fast. Help us to use our time wisely as you make us into the creation we will be for eternity. In Jesus' most holy name we pray, Amen.

Day 21

Praise the LORD. Praise the LORD, my soul. I will praise the LORD all my life; I will sing praise to my God as long as I live. Do not put your trust in princes, in human beings, who cannot save. When their spirit departs, they return to the ground; on that very day their plans come to nothing. Blessed are those whose help is the God of Jacob, whose hope is in the LORD their God. He is the Maker of heaven and earth, the sea, and everything in them— he remains faithful forever. – Psalm 146: 1-6

There are so many reasons for us to give praise to the Lord. He is our Creator, our Redeemer, the One who gives us eternal life. He is the One who will never leave us or forsake us. Humans will fail us – guaranteed. Even those most dear to us, will fail us at some point. We get let down, disappointed, frustrated, sad, etc. when this happens. However, let this be a reminder to us that our trust should be in the Lord alone, and He is faithful!

Prayer: We thank you, Lord, that you are faithful forever! Because we are in a broken, sinful world, no one can be that perfect person for us. Only you can fill the void we are so longingly looking to fill.

Help us to be thankful for the relationships you've put in our lives while recognizing when we may be expecting too much from these relationships. Help us to continually look to you as our source of grace, strength, wisdom, peace, and mercy so that we can offer grace and mercy to the ones who are in our lives. We ask this in Jesus' name, Amen.

Day 22

Therefore, my dear friends, as you have always obeyed—not only in my presence, but now much more in my absence—continue to work out your salvation with fear and trembling, for it is God who works in you to will and to act in order to fulfill his good purpose. – Philippians 2:12-13

What does it mean to work out our salvation with fear and trembling? It means to have awe and reverence to our God who has redeemed us. The moment we were saved through believing in our Savior, Jesus Christ, we became a new creation. As one of the earlier prayers in this book stated, we have been justified through our faith in the Lord Jesus Christ. Once we accept Him, we receive the gift of eternal life immediately. Once this happens, we begin the process of sanctification – becoming more Christlike – and here is where we have to actively work towards this. We do this by obeying our Lord's Words and staying close to Him so that He can renew our hearts and minds. We also trust Him that He can do this work in us. Because it is God who works in us to will and to act in order to fulfill His good purpose!

Prayer: Thank you, Lord, that you have given us all we need for salvation – and when we receive this gift - you have given us the eternal security of this salvation! We thank you that you are working in us all the time to will and to act in order to fulfill your good purpose. May we be mindful of this truth, and may we trust you to empower us to do what you have entrusted to us. We ask that you remind us of your promises and that we depend on you to help us obey and do all that you require of us. Thank you so much for allowing us to take part in your heavenly kingdom work – what an honor! We ask this in Jesus' precious name, Amen.

Day 23

But seek first his kingdom and his righteousness, and all these things will be given to you as well. Therefore do not worry about tomorrow, for tomorrow will worry about itself. Each day has enough trouble of its own. – Matthew 6:33-34

There are many cares in this world. There are troubles as well. However, our Lord told us that if we seek Him and the ways of Him (His Kingdom) and His righteousness, which is only found in Him, we will have all we need. Our loving God provides for us in all the ways we need – both physical and spiritual. It's amazing how we see this so clearly when we put our trust in Him when the world would give us every reason not to. We're going to have concerns, but it's what we do when these concerns arise that make the difference. Do we trust in our God who can provide all things or do we get overwhelmed by the cares of the world and operate in unbelief?

Prayer: Father, we thank you that you are our Provider, our Comforter. Help us to rest in the security we have in you. We are to cast our anxieties on you because you care for us. Help us to remember this truth and to rest in the peace of knowing that we can't be any safer or in a better place than resting in our faith and trust in You. We ask this in Jesus' name, Amen.

Day 24

See, I will create new heavens and a new earth. The former things will not be remembered, nor will they come to mind. But be glad and rejoice forever in what I will create, for I will create Jerusalem to be a delight and its people a joy. I will rejoice over Jerusalem and take delight in my people; the sound of weeping and of crying will be heard in it no more. – Isaiah 65:17-19; Then I saw "a new heaven and a new earth," for the first heaven and the first earth had passed away, and there was no longer any sea. I saw the Holy City, the new Jerusalem, coming down out of heaven from God, prepared as a bride beautifully dressed for her husband. And I heard a loud voice from the throne saying, "Look! God's dwelling place is now among the people and he will dwell with them. They will be his people, and God himself will be with them and be their God. 'He will wipe every tear from their eyes. There will be no more death or mourning or crying or pain, for the old order of things has passed away." – Revelation 21:1-4

Wow, we have such an amazing future waiting for us! Our amazing God – the God of the universe – will dwell among us! There IS coming a day when He will make all things new and will wipe away all of our tears, pain, and illness. There will be no more death or mourning. How amazing that His Word, which is contained in the supernatural book we call the Bible, speaks about this new heaven and new earth in the writings listed above that were written over 700 years apart from each other! This is not a fairy tale. Our Lord – King of Kings – is coming again, He is going to rule and reign forever, and we get to be a part of His kingdom by believing and hoping in Him. Truly amazing!

Prayer: Lord, we thank you for what you have planned for those who love you. Eye has not seen, ear has not heard these plans, but you know them. Jesus, you told us that you were going away to prepare a place for us and if it weren't true you wouldn't tell it. We thank you that you are real, you do have amazing plans for us (both now and eternally), and we ask that you would help us to have the courage and the wisdom to reveal your truths to all that we come in contact with so that they too can choose to spend eternity in the amazing place you have prepared for us. We ask this in the mighty name of Jesus, Amen.

Day 25

I will exalt you, LORD, for you lifted me out of the depths and did not let my enemies gloat over me. LORD my God, I called to you for help, and you healed me. You, LORD, brought me up from the realm of the dead; you spared me from going down to the pit. Sing the praises of the LORD, you his faithful people; praise his holy name. For his anger lasts only a moment, but his favor lasts a lifetime; weeping may stay for the night, but rejoicing comes in the morning – Psalm 30:1-5

When we call to God for help, He always answers. We may not understand all of the ways that He works for He sees what we do not; however, He is working in a way that will ultimately bring good to us – both now and for eternity. When we cry out to Him to save us, he offers us a salvation that not only spares us from the pit but brings us joy everlasting. Down through the ages, beginning with ancient Israel, God has offered His people mercy. He is a just God, and He does have holy anger, but His mercy and favor He shows us, by offering His Son, lasts forever. We may have weeping at times during the night (our earthly life) but rejoicing will come in the morning (eternity).

Prayer: Lord, we do praise you; we praise your holy name! We thank you that we can call to you in our pain and sickness and you do heal us. You offer us hope now and you work in amazing ways in our lives, but you are ultimately working for us for our place forever with you in eternity. Thank you for the favor you bestow on us! We ask that you keep us mindful of this greater work that you are doing in us. In Jesus' name we pray, Amen.

Day 26

Let them give thanks to the LORD for his unfailing love and his wonderful deeds for mankind...– Psalm 107:8; Now on his way to Jerusalem, Jesus traveled along the border between Samaria and Galilee. As he was going into a village, ten men who had leprosy met him. They stood at a distance and called out in a loud voice, "Jesus, Master, have pity on us!" When he saw them, he said, "Go, show yourselves to the priests." And as they went, they were cleansed. One of them, when he saw he was healed, came back, praising God in a loud voice. He threw himself at Jesus' feet and thanked him—and he was a Samaritan. Jesus asked, "Were not all ten cleansed? Where are the other nine? Has no one returned to give praise to God except this foreigner?" Then he said to him, "Rise and go; your faith has made you well." – Luke 17:11-17

Jesus healed ten lepers, and only one returned to give thanks! Are we thankful for all of the things He has done in our lives? First, He has forgiven us our sins and given us eternal life. This would be enough to give Him thanksgiving - often! However, He continues to work in our lives to bless us, provide for us, heal us, counsel us, the list goes on and on. Our Lord desires that we would give Him thanks. An interesting thing happens when we give Him thanks – we feel joy! Let us continually offer thanks to our God for everything He has done and will do for us!

Prayer: Oh precious Father, thank you so much, first, for who you are! Thank you for the amazing gifts you bestow on us, your children! Forgive us when we fail to thank you for all that you've done for us. We want you to know how thankful we really are. We want to be like the one leper who threw himself down at Jesus' feet and thanked Him with a loud voice. Let our voices continue to boldly thank our Triune God! In Jesus' most holy name we pray, Amen.

Day 27

Don't you have a saying, 'It's still four months until harvest'? I tell you, open your eyes and look at the fields! They are ripe for harvest. Even now the one who reaps draws a wage and harvests a crop for eternal life, so that the sower and the reaper may be glad together. Thus the saying 'One sows and another reaps' is true. I sent you to reap what you have not worked for. Others have done the hard work, and you have reaped the benefits of their labor."– John 4:35-38

These words of truth, spoken by our Savior, remind us that there are sowers and reapers, and they are both glad. We can become discouraged when it seems like all of our efforts to lead people to the Lord appear to have failed. However, we may be the ones sowing the seeds, and someone else gets to see the harvest. There may be times where we get to reap what someone else has toiled for. Either way, we need to remember that the fields are ripe for harvest and it is our honor to take part in our King's work and to help bring more people into His Kingdom. Whether we sow or reap, we will rejoice when we are able to see the ultimate harvest in heaven.

Prayer: We thank you, Lord that you have blessed us with the honor of harvesting for your Kingdom. We ask that you help us to not become discouraged when we aren't able to see our loved ones or friends come to you the way we'd like. Helps us to remember that some are sowers and others are reapers, but that we all will rejoice together when we're able to see the harvest in heaven. Give us the strength and the courage to boldly work for the ultimate harvest. We ask this in Jesus' name, Amen.

Day 28

*I thank him who has given me strength, Christ Jesus our Lord, because he judged me faithful, appointing me to his service, though formerly I was a blasphemer, persecutor, and insolent opponent. But I received mercy because I had acted ignorantly in unbelief, and the grace of our Lord overflowed for me with the faith and love that are in Christ Jesus. The saying is trustworthy and deserving of full acceptance, that Christ Jesus came into the world to save sinners, of whom I am the foremost. But I received mercy for this reason, that in me, as the foremost, Jesus Christ might display his perfect patience as an example to those who were to believe in him for eternal life. To the King of the ages, immortal, invisible, the only God, be honor and glory forever and ever. Amen.–
1 Timothy 1:12-17*

The apostle Paul talks here of his thankfulness to our Lord in the way He showed mercy on him and was able to use him for the kingdom. He talks about his former self as a blasphemer, persecutor, and insolent opponent. Sound a lot different than how we may have lived our lives before we accepted Christ? Paul says that Christ came into the world to save sinners, and he talks about how Christ was able to use him

(Paul) as an example to bring more people to believe in Jesus Christ for eternal life.

Wow, Paul has definitely been used to bring others to belief in Jesus! The message for us is that the grace and love that flows from our Savior to us who believe changes us so that we too may be an example to bring others to belief in Christ. No matter how badly we may have sinned or messed things up (we may think), if we put our hope and trust in the Lord, he not only gives us salvation and eternal life, but He can use us to bring others to this gift as well. That's definitely purpose in life – no matter who we are.

Prayer: Lord, we thank you once again for all that you do for us. We thank you that you can and do use broken people to aid you in bringing about your purposes. Help us to not take the honor that you have bestowed upon us to further your kingdom lightly. For everyone who calls Jesus their Savior, they are given a mighty purpose and role in this life that will be rewarded in eternity – the role of sharing His free gift of salvation to others. Lord, help us find satisfaction and joy in this mighty work you have called us to do and have graciously entrusted to us. We ask this in Jesus' precious name, Amen.

Day 29

When Jesus spoke again to the people, he said, "I am the light of the world. Whoever follows me will never walk in darkness, but will have the light of life."– *John 8:12*

When we are in the dark, we can't see anything. It's a scary place. It's hard to see images, and they sometimes look completely different than what they really are in the light. But, when you flip on the light switch, everything comes into focus, and what seemed scary disappears. Because we are in a broken, sinful world, we do not have the light we need in order to see the way we should. Our Lord is light. His presence in our lives shines the light on the dark parts of our world as well as within ourselves. When we trust in Him, He opens our eyes and gives us new perspective with which we can view our circumstances and ourselves. He enables us to see our need for a Savior and then He walks with us through this life allowing us to be shielded by His light, which protects us and guides us on the path that He would have for us. His light ultimately leads us to eternal life – with Him!

Prayer: Thank you, Jesus, that you are the light of the world! We thank you that you are the light that shines the way for us so that we aren't in darkness. We ask that you would help us to see even more clearly by allowing more of your light in our lives. The more of you we have, the more light we have for which to see and be powered by. This requires us to stay closely connected to you. Lord, hold on tightly to us! We ask this in Jesus' name, Amen.

Day 30

My goal is that they may be encouraged in heart and united in love, so that they may have the full riches of complete understanding, in order that they may know the mystery of God, namely, Christ, in whom are hidden all the treasures of wisdom and knowledge.– *Colossians 2:2-3*

In Christ is really everything we need. He holds all the wisdom and knowledge we need for both this life and the eternal life to come. The truth is that we really can't think the thoughts we need to think, act in the way we need to act or really do anything that is pleasing to Him apart from Him. However, with Him, we can do the impossible. Sometimes the impossible is just managing our own internal battles. However, because we have the Holy Spirit within us, we have the mind of Christ, who can instruct us and guide us in all things. (*For who has known the mind of the Lord that he may instruct him?" But we have the mind of Christ. – 1 Corinthians 2: 16.*)

Prayer: Wow, we are so thankful, Lord, to you who have given us all things in your Son, Jesus! Triune, majestic, amazing God, how can it be that you not only offer us salvation and the most amazing eternity planned for us, but you also give us your powerful, beautiful Spirit to live inside of us so that we would be connected to you! Through your Holy Spirit, we are guided, comforted, and spoken to by you. We ask, Lord, that you would help us so that we won't grieve the Holy Spirit, with Whom we are sealed for the day of redemption, and that you would forgive us when we've chosen the worldly way over your way. Help us to remember the real power we have within by being your child. We ask this in Jesus' precious name, Amen.

Day 31

Jesus answered, "I am the way and the truth and the life. No one comes to the Father except through me.- John 14:6

This pretty much sums it up, doesn't it? The words "no one" mean that not one person, *not one*, can come to the Father except through Jesus. As the way, only Jesus can provide the path to salvation. As the truth, Jesus is the incarnate Word of God, and is the SOURCE of all truth. By contrast, the devil is the father of lies, and the world wants us to believe those lies - lies like, "Truth is relative" or "There are many paths to God, etc." There was only one human being who came to earth, died, and rose again on the third day, and the world, in addition to individuals, was forever changed! That human being was both man and God – Jesus Christ. This Jesus gives us deliverance from a life of bondage to sin and death to a life of freedom in eternity.

Prayer: Thank you, Jesus, that you came to provide the way for us out of bondage to the sin that ensnares everyone on earth and that you lead us into the only truth – your truth. We thank you that you came to give us life, and life to the fullest, both now and forever. We can never thank you enough. We ask that we will be always mindful of the treasure you are and will continually praise you for everything you've done and continue to do for us. Help us to boldly share your truth with those who don't know you so that they too would know the way, the truth and the life. In Jesus' name we pray, Amen.

Day 32

All those the Father gives me will come to me, and whoever comes to me I will never drive away. For I have come down from heaven not to do my will but to do the will of him who sent me. And this is the will of him who sent me, that I shall lose none of all those he has given me, but raise them up at the last day. For my Father's will is that everyone who looks to the Son and believes in him shall have eternal life, and I will raise them up at the last day. – John 6:37-40

How amazing is it that it's God's will that everyone who looks to His Son and believes in Him will have eternal life and that He will keep us to Himself and protect us so that we will be brought home to heaven in eternity with Him! Being aware of this truth, we should be encouraged that the Lord is keeping us and that He who began a good work in us will carry it on to completion until the day of Christ Jesus (Philippians 1:6). Let us not be princes and princesses in rags who don't know the truth of Who we belong to and what our inheritance is! When we understand this truth, we will act accordingly in the ways He would have us - both with confidence and with the right motives.

Prayer: Thank you Lord that you have chosen us and that when we say "Yes" to you that you keep us and protect us on our journey through life and then you bring us home safely to eternity with you. Let us meditate on this truth so that we will be encouraged and know that we are eternally yours and that you are working within us. We ask that you would open our eyes so that we would understand how amazing this truth is like we have never before understood. Help us to act in a way that is befitting of one who is the recipient of such a gift. Help us to understand the treasure you are! Let this truth drive away any unwarranted fears and allow us to live bold lives for you. We ask that you would give us divine appointments so that we can share this amazing truth with others. In Jesus' most holy name we pray, Amen.

Day 33

I am the bread of life. Your ancestors ate the manna in the wilderness, yet they died. But here is the bread that comes down from heaven, which anyone may eat and not die. I am the living bread that came down from heaven. Whoever eats this bread will live forever. This bread is my flesh, which I will give for the life of the world." - John 6:48-51

Jesus is the "the way, the truth and the life" and no one can come to the Father except through Him. Salvation is provided only through belief in the One who died on the cross for our sins. Not only did Jesus provide the way for eternal life, He has given us a way to overcome our troubles in this life by feeding on Him and His word. Jesus is the Word. The way for us to know Him is to be in a relationship with Him. A relationship requires a two-way exchange. When we talk with Him and share our lives with Him, He responds. Sometimes it's that faint stirring within us that offers direction or peace. Other times, He speaks directly to us through His Word. In fact, it's through His Word that we know His thoughts and ideas. When we read it, meditate on it and store it within us, He will bring it back to us at the right time in order for us to apply it to the situation or circumstance. Sometimes He causes certain scriptures to stand out at a particular time. However He chooses to do it, it all begins with His Word. If we want to grow in our relationship with Him, we need to let Him speak to us through His Word.

Prayer: Heavenly Father, we thank you for your Word! Just like we need food to nourish our bodies and to fortify us, we need our Lord Jesus (the Word) to nourish, sustain and fortify our souls. We ask that we would grow closer to you and that you would give us an even greater desire to know your Word and to plant it deeply within us. We ask this in Jesus' name, Amen.

Day 34

For there is one God and one mediator between God and mankind, the man Christ Jesus, who gave himself as a ransom for all people. This has now been witnessed to at the proper time. - 1 Timothy 2:12-17

The dictionary defines a mediator as one who settles a dispute or brings about an agreement or truce between parties. Because of the huge separation between man and God due to sin, which every person has, there needed to be a way to build a bridge between God and us. Jesus is that bridge. He is the one that reconciles us back to God by our belief in Him. He also now sits at the right hand of God and intercedes for us (Romans 8:34).

Prayer: Thank you, precious Jesus, that you are the great Mediator between us and our majestic God! We thank you that you are love incarnate. You who had everything, and all things were made through you, chose to come to earth to pay our ransom so that we could be made right to stand before our Holy God. We thank you that you continue to intercede for us as we walk along our journey on earth. We ask that we would understand this reality for what it is so that we would both be thankful and empowered. We ask this in Jesus' precious name, Amen.

Day 35

The next day the great crowd that had come for the festival heard that Jesus was on his way to Jerusalem. They took palm branches and went out to meet him, shouting, "Hosanna!" "Blessed is he who comes in the name of the Lord!" "Blessed is the king of Israel!" Jesus found a young donkey and sat on it, as it is written: "Do not be afraid, Daughter Zion; see, your king is coming, seated on a donkey's colt." At first his disciples did not understand all this. Only after Jesus was glorified did they realize that these things had been written about him and that these things had been done to him. – John 12:12-16

Throughout the Old Testament, promises of the Messiah were given. Prophesies of Jesus, often called the Messianic Prophesies, were made hundreds, sometimes thousands of years, before Jesus was born. The bible is the only book that has accurately predicted the future. The future is still yet to come, but we know our Lord is going to come back again and will be the eternal King since His Word tells us so. The people of Jesus' time who knew the scriptures would have known that Zechariah 9:9, quoted in the above passage about the colt, was about the Messiah, and they appeared to believe He was the one at this moment in history. However, things changed substantially as He took His walk to the cross, and even His disciples didn't seem to understand what was happening. However, after Jesus was glorified, they realized that these things had been written about Him. Let this be an example to us to not miss what might be happening in our time in fulfillment of prophesies and to trust that His future promises to us are true, even if we don't understand it all now.

Prayer: We thank you, Father, that you have given us your Word to guide us and give us hope. We thank you that you have supernaturally preserved your Word so that we can look back and see how you have worked throughout history and how you have fulfilled your promises to us and will continue to do so. We are so thankful for our beloved Savior, who so gently comes in such majesty and authority! Help us learn from Him as we go about our lives in humble service to you. We ask this in Jesus' name, Amen.

Day 36

Jesus entered the temple courts and drove out all who were buying and selling there. He overturned the tables of the money changers and the benches of those selling doves. "It is written," he said to them, "'My house will be called a house of prayer, but you are making it 'a den of robbers.' –Matthew 21: 12-13

Righteous anger. This is what our Lord had upon seeing what the people were doing in the place that was supposed to be for worship of the Lord. We too should be angry when we see the things that anger our God. However, there is a way for us to manage anger. We are instructed, "In your anger, do not sin" (Ephesians 4:26). Many times, our anger results from petty arguments or personal slights – this is not righteous anger. However, when we are angered by the injustices we see in our world that are in direct opposition to the things of God, we should be motivated by our righteous anger to do something. By doing something, we should pray for God's wisdom and seek His Word first, and then go about doing what He would have us do to spread His love and forgiveness to a broken, sinful world.

Prayer: We thank you, Lord, that because of Who you are – loving, merciful, holy – you are angered by injustice and sin. The anger you have comes out of your genuine love for your creation and your concern for our spiritual condition. We ask that by your Holy Spirit, you would help us be sensitive to the things you care about and to break our hearts for what breaks yours. Guide us where you would have us go and what you would have us do to spread your love and forgiveness to this broken world we live in. We ask this in Jesus' precious name, Amen.

Day 37

When he had finished washing their feet, he put on his clothes and returned to his place. "Do you understand what I have done for you?" he asked them. "You call me 'Teacher' and 'Lord,' and rightly so, for that is what I am. Now that I, your Lord and Teacher, have washed your feet, you also should wash one another's feet. I have set you an example that you should do as I have done for you. Very truly I tell you, no servant is greater than his master, nor is a messenger greater than the one who sent him. Now that you know these things, you will be blessed if you do them - John 13:12-17

The washing of the disciples' feet was a profound example our Lord gave us. Dirty (possibly stinky) feet are not the most desirous thing. In fact, this service was the work of the lowliest of servants in Jesus' time. However, Jesus, God incarnate, stooped to the feet of His disciples in an act that foreshadowed the ultimate act of humility and love that He displayed on the cross. Our precious Savior came to earth not to be served but to serve and give His life as a ransom for many (Matthew 20:28).

As His followers, we too are to live a life of service and humility as we follow our Master's example.

Prayer: Thank you, Lord Jesus, that you – the King of kings – and Lord of lords - humbled yourself and came to earth to pay the ransom for us so that we could have eternal life with you. Who or what other religion can offer us that? None! We ask that you would help us remember your example of humility as we walk along on our journeys in life so that we would live in such a way that we would be able to point others to you. We want our lights to so shine before men that they will see our good deeds and give glory to you! In Jesus' name we pray, Amen.

Day 38

While they were eating, Jesus took bread, and when he had given thanks, he broke it and gave it to his disciples, saying, "Take and eat; this is my body." Then he took a cup, and when he had given thanks, he gave it to them, saying, "Drink from it, all of you. This is my blood of the covenant, which is poured out for many for the forgiveness of sins. – Matthew 26: 26-27

There's a saying that Jesus is in the Old Testament concealed and in the New Testament revealed. The Passover celebration was in remembrance of God's deliverance of Israel out of Egypt. The word "Passover" was from when the Lord passed over all the houses that had the blood of the lamb on the doorposts so that the death of every first-born (the tenth of the plagues the Lord sent on Egypt) would not come on them. Jesus instituted the Lord's Supper on the Passover since the Passover was really a foreshadowing of the Lamb of God (Jesus) who, by His death and resurrection, allows for us to be passed over when it comes to judgment from God. The interesting thing about the Passover was that it didn't matter if the doorpost that had blood on it was a Jewish home or an Egyptian one, as long as there was blood, they were "passed over". In the same way, whether Gentile or Jew, if we have the blood of the Lamb (by believing in Jesus), we will be saved.

Prayer: Thank you, Lord, for your love for us! Just like you executed judgment in the days of Israel's enslavement in Egypt on the unrighteous yet spared those who had the blood on the doorposts (even if they were Egyptians), you too will spare us if we believe on your beloved Son – our Precious Savior – the true Lamb of God! It doesn't matter who we are, where we came from or what we've done, if we have the blood of the Lamb on us by believing in Him, we will be spared from your righteous judgment and given an amazing gift of eternity with you - our amazing God and giver of all good things! We ask that you would give us opportunities to share this amazing love you have for us and that you would help us to remember, always be thankful and grow closer to our source of life – Jesus our Lord. In Jesus' most holy name we pray, Amen.

Day 39

*Going a little farther, he fell with his face to the ground and prayed, "My Father, if it is possible, may this cup be taken from me. Yet not as I will, but as you will. - **Matthew 26:39***

Imagine what our Lord went though at this moment in time. He was both man and God. Being God, He knew exactly all of the events that would take place. He knew the suffering He would have to endure both physically, and probably worst of all, spiritually when He was separated from His triune relationship with God the Father when He bore all of our sins on Himself and God had to look away. There is nothing worse in the entire universe than separation from God. Because our God is holy, He cannot look on sin. How amazing that God provided a way for us to be right with Him and considered righteous so that we wouldn't be separated from Him. That way cost Him great suffering, though – let us never forget that!

Prayer: Heavenly Father, we thank you for your redemptive plan for mankind! You knew before the beginning of the world what would happen with fallen man and what you would need to do to offer a way back to you. That plan cost you greatly and yet it gained for us who received the gift everything! We can never thank you enough! We want you to know how thankful we are to you our amazing, loving, merciful God. We ask that you would deepen our faith in our Lord Jesus and that we would desire nothing as much as our relationship with Him. We ask this in Jesus' name, Amen.

Day 40

Surely he took up our pain and bore our suffering, yet we considered him punished by God, stricken by him, and afflicted. But he was pierced for our transgressions, he was crushed for our iniquities; the punishment that brought us peace was on him, and by his wounds we are healed. We all, like sheep, have gone astray, each of us has turned to our own way; and the LORD has laid on him the iniquity of us all. – Isaiah 53:5-6

There is not one person who is alive now or ever was that was not sinful - except for Jesus Christ. However, "God made him who had no sin to be sin for us, so that in him we might become the righteousness of God" (1 Corinthians 5:21). What parent, if their child was going to be executed, wouldn't want to take their place? This is what our God did for us. He took the punishment that belonged to us out of His love and compassion for us. His word tells us that if we being evil (sinful) people know how to give good gifts to our children, how much more our heavenly Father gives to us who ask. All He requires of us to be right with Him is to ask Him into our hearts and to believe in Him. As we meditate on the life of our Savior and the death He endured for us on that cross, let us never stop thanking Him, our God – the perfect Father!

Prayer: Thank you, Heavenly Father, for your unending love for us! You who did not spare you Own Son but gave Him up for us, how amazing you are! We fall down before you in thanksgiving and praise and ask that our worship of you will honor you as you so deserve. We ask that we will be forever changed in that we will be even closer to you – our love, our life - and that we will grow in the grace and knowledge of our Lord and Savior Jesus Christ. We ask that by the power of your Holy Spirit we would live our lives in a way that would be pleasing to you and that we would grow even deeper in our love for you. We ask this in the powerful and precious name of our Savior, Jesus Christ, Amen.

Closing Thoughts

The scripture from Day 40 (Isaiah 53:5-6) was written around 700 years before Jesus was born and before crucifixion was invented. (*But he was pierced for our transgressions, he was crushed for our iniquities; the punishment that brought us peace was on him, and by his wounds we are healed.*) Isn't that amazing? In fact, Psalm 22, which many believe to be a direct prophesy about Jesus and his crucifixion, was written *1000* years before the event happened. Psalm 22:16-18 states: *Dogs surround me, a pack of villains encircles me; they pierce my hands and my feet. All my bones are on display; people stare and gloat over me. They divide my clothes among them and cast lots for my garment.* In the New Testament, Matthew records what happens when the Roman soldiers divide Jesus' clothes: *When they had crucified him, they divided up his clothes by casting lots* (Matthew 27:35).

The Bible really is a supernatural book that has prophesied many things that have come to happen. Concerning Jesus, some scholars put the number of prophesies about Him in the Old Testament in the hundreds. There are many other prophesies that have come to be and many more that still will be fulfilled in the future. I mention this since my own faith has been strengthened by my study of the Bible and the historical evidence that supports the truth of it.

Before I ever studied the Bible for myself, I admit that I had often wondered if it was all really true or if maybe some of it was just myth. However, unlike mythology, the Bible contains many prophesies that have come true. Also, unlike mythology, events and people in the Bible can be historically verified. Importantly, the Bible has transformed a countless number of lives.

I could end this book with more discussion and evidence about the historicity of the Bible, but the truth is it's up to each person to honestly investigate for themselves. For those who are reading this book and have not accepted Jesus or His Word, I urge you to do it. It's the most important thing you will ever do. If you want to give your life to the Lord right this moment, you can say this prayer:

> *Dear Jesus, I know that I am a sinner and need your forgiveness. I believe that you died on the cross for my sins and rose from the grave to give me life. I know you are the only way to God, so now I want to quit*

disobeying you and start living for you. Please forgive me, change my life and show me how to know you. In Jesus' name. Amen.

If this is your sincere prayer, angels are rejoicing in heaven! You now have the Holy Spirit of the living God inside of you! God's free gift of salvation is that easy. It's free! It's not about religion, it's about what *He* did for you and the relationship He wants to have with you both now and forever. Read His Word (the Bible). A good place to start is the Gospel of Mark. Talk with Him and make Him part of all you do. Get connected with others who also are walking with Him. Let Him give you the abundant life He so wants to give you – both now and forever!

Very truly I tell you, whoever hears my word and believes him who sent me has eternal life and will not be judged but has crossed over from death to life. - John 5:24

Salvation is found in no one else, for there is no other name under heaven given to mankind by which we must be saved. – Acts 4:12

The thief comes only to steal and kill and destroy; I have come that they may have life, and have it to the full. - John 10:10

Additional Reading

If you want to know more about Jesus and the Bible, here are some books and websites that I found very helpful:

Books

The Case for Faith: A Journalist Investigates the Toughest Objections to Christianity by Lee Strobel

Mere Christianity by C.S. Lewis

Websites

Bible Gateway: www.biblegateway.com

Christ Notes: www.christnotes.com

Got Questions Ministries: www.gotquestions.org